# A Proverb & A Question

C.J. Ward

ISBN: 978-1-365-56910-4

## DEDICATION

This book is dedicated to my beautiful (& extremely loving) sister, Tonia – thank you for sharing your unconditional love with me throughout the years and I appreciate your willingness to always try to be there for me! In life, I have recognized the importance of wisdom and understanding during our journey through life. I believe, and I think you'll agree with me, family is the foundation; however, the members of the family have to be wise/understanding enough to play their part – family is everything!

Love you Sis,

C.J. Ward

"Wisdom is the precursor to understanding your destiny, and knowledge is the key to building a long-lasting legacy"

~ C.J. Ward

## *Proverbs 1*

**<u>Question</u>**: Wise counsel…has it called out to you lately? If so, how did you respond to it; with rejection or acceptance?

Reply/Thoughts:

***Author's Notes:***

*Personally, I received some very wise advice recently that I could have accepted or rejected. Looking back at certain seasons in my life I couldn't help but notice the times when I would have rejected such advice/counsel; however due to increased wisdom and understanding over the years…I'm now able to recognize the nonsense that is often attached to pride. I truly thank GOD for this revelation!*

### *Proverb 2*

**Question**: Based on this proverb…how does someone tune their ears to wisdom and concentrate on understanding?

Reply/Thoughts:

***Author's Notes:***

*In my opinion, I believe it all begins with...pursuing a relationship with GOD (v.4). While pursuing a relationship with GOD you will begin to experience new ways of thinking and a new passion to live a more GOD-centered way of life (v.5). Once a relationship with GOD is truly established, you will recognize His purpose(s) all around you; through the Word, the HOLY SPIRIT, people, circumstances, situations, and through prayer (v.6). Wisdom comes along with experiencing GOD. Thank you LORD for wisdom and understanding, and I'm faithful to receive more in due time!!!*

### *Proverbs 3*

This proverb is filled with an abundance of wisdom. However, I would like to concentrate on three particular verses today (***Proverbs 3:3, 5-6***). So with these verses in mind, I will present you with two questions:

**Question #1** (***Proverbs 3:3***): What attributes are you holding on to? Based on your response; would you be content in wearing those attributes around your neck for representation? Better yet…do they convey the same message that is in your heart?

**Question #2** (***Proverbs 3:5-6***): What is more important; GOD's Will or your own understanding?

Reply/Thoughts:

***Author's Notes:***

*Transparently speaking; currently, I'm holding on to some attributes that are good and bad. Those that are good I count it all joy, however the ones I consider to be bad I'm focusing on killing them by faith and/or dying spiritually daily (killing the selfish and prideful desires of the flesh; basically, my sinful nature (see* ***Romans 7:7-25****). Although my attributes aren't all good, I would be content to wear them around my neck because I believe it would reveal to the lost souls of world that I'm truly not perfect nor do I think I am. Also, I believe it would minister to them that although they may have many flaws…GOD will receive them where they are if they're willing to pursue a relationship with Him. Helping and ministering to others is in my heart, so I hope my walk and the attributes I wear around my neck communicates the same message. I would have to answer, absolutely GOD's Will. However, saying it and living it are two totally different things. I thank GOD for His patient love, because I'm beginning to understand how to distinguish; walking a path per my own understanding and following a path directed by GOD's Will.*

## *Proverbs 4*

**Question**: Which path would you prefer; one that is well-lit or one that is dark?

Reply/Thoughts:

***Author's Notes:***

*In my opinion, I believe the answer is obvious; however, I think we tend to make this question more difficult than it should be…if we refer solely on our actions. Righteousness/Light or Wickedness/Darkness; this is the choice. I don't know about you but I would rather walk around a well-lit room at night and avoid possibly stumping my toe (bad decisions) or tripping over a piece of furniture (stumbling/falling), than trying to make my way around in the dark. When I look at things with this perspective, I believe the decision is very simple…choose the path of righteousness.*

## *Proverbs 5*

**Question**: Which path(s) have you decided to take?

Reply/Thoughts:

***Author's Notes:***

*Personally, this proverb could not have come at a better time. As I have often shared, I don't mind being transparent at all if it's for a greater good. I truly believe a ministry can be found within a testimony, and the truth will set you free. So, with that said; the mistakes and the fears of my yesterdays will no longer impact my path(s) of today and tomorrow. Self-bondage will only hold you captive as long as you allow it to…and today, I have decided to drop my chains. Hear me loud and clear, I don't express this pledge to receive praise or to be admired…I share this publicly because I'm real about my walk and my witness. Discernment comes with wisdom, and wisdom creates better decision-making…find wisdom and cherish it!*

## *Proverbs 6*

**Question**: What has GOD been telling you to do? Has it been done? If not, what are you waiting for?

Reply/Thoughts:

***Author's Notes:***

*Personally, GOD has been telling me to do many certain things for a while now. Have they been accomplished? No, not all…but a few of them have been pursued as of lately. However, speaking with all the honesty in my heart, the only reason I've hesitated in pursuing most, if not all of them, has been due to fear. And I can now honestly say; I've been waiting on becoming fearless in order to fulfill GOD's purpose(s) for my life. Well, as Sam Cooke once shared in a very fond song to my spirit, A Change is Gonna Come; in reference to my walk and my life…it has arrived! I speak this in the name of the LORD! It's time! Thank You LORD for the sense of urgency!!!*

***Proverbs 7***

*I would like to point out that this proverb definitely applies to women as well and not just to men.* So with this in mind; let us all love wisdom unconditionally like a brother or sister (as a brother would protect his sister from harm or the way a sister would guard her brother from trouble) and adopt insight into our lives as if it was a part of us since birth.

**Question**: What has wisdom or insight protected you from lately?

Reply/Thoughts:

______________________________________________

______________________________________________

______________________________________________

______________________________________________

______________________________________________

______________________________________________

______________________________________________

______________________________________________

______________________________________________

______________________________________________

______________________________________________

______________________________________________

______________________________________________

______________________________________________

______________________________________________

______________________________________________

______________________________________________

______________________________________________

___________________________________________

___________________________________________

***Author's Notes:***

*Personally, wisdom and insight have guarded me from myself. Better yet, they have guarded me from my own understanding. I thank GOD for giving me the wisdom of knowing how much I really don't know. I must depend on GOD for everything!!!*

***Proverbs 8***

Ahh…there are so many things I would like to touch on within this passage, however I will refrain from doing what I would like to do and go with what my spirit is telling me to concentrate on.

**Question**: In the company of wisdom and good judgment you will also experience the presence of common sense, insight, and success. However, in the company of pride and arrogance; corruption and conversations of perverse speech will fill the air. If you had to choose, which gathering would you like to attend? (*Don't just go with the obvious selection because of how it sounds…really think about it for a moment and assess the circles you've been a part of lately*)

Reply/Thoughts:

______________________________________________

______________________________________________

______________________________________________

______________________________________________

______________________________________________

______________________________________________

______________________________________________

______________________________________________

______________________________________________

______________________________________________

______________________________________________

______________________________________________

______________________________________________

______________________________________________

_______________________________________________________

_______________________________________________________

***Author's Notes:***

*Personally, I've been in the company of both parties at various times of my life. However, today, tomorrow, and until my entire body ceases functioning altogether; I will choose to be in the company of wisdom and good judgment. Think about it; in the company of pride and arrogance the entire conversation will be centered on self: "I did this…and I did that. I'm the sole reason behind my success. I've outgrown GOD (I couldn't resist…I had to include it; this particular individual knows what I'm referring to). I, I, I, I…" But if you're in the company of wisdom and good judgment; I visualize the conversation going more like; "Without GOD, I wouldn't be here today." I really don't need to expand any further than that statement, because without the natural-life GOD has given all of us so unconditionally…neither conversation would be able to exist. Pride and arrogance often shares that money and riches are everything (in this world I believe money has its purpose, but I don't believe it's everything), but wisdom and good judgment ensures me that GOD is everything. I thank GOD for His constant blessings of knowledge!!!*

****natural**-life ~ the life everyone has through natural birth; not the eternal-life you must choose to have through Christ…*

***Proverbs 9***

**Question**: Are you ready for a lengthier life? If so, search for wisdom by pursuing a relationship with Christ first.

Reply/Thoughts:

________________________________________________________________________________

________________________________________________________________________________

________________________________________________________________________________

________________________________________________________________________________

________________________________________________________________________________

***Author's Notes:***

*Personally, I'm all in!!*

***Proverbs 10***

**Question**: How grounded are you in Christ?

Reply/Thoughts:

______________________________________________

______________________________________________

______________________________________________

______________________________________________

______________________________________________

***Author's Notes:***

*In my opinion, without Christ…my foundation is non-existent. As I continue to mature as a human being and grow more in Christ; I'm realizing more and more that the LORD is the only thing concrete being in my life. Materials will come and go while people are like the wind, but my dependence in the LORD is like an unmovable anchor (see* ***Hebrews 6:13-20****). Thank you LORD for being the One I can depend on during good times and bad!!!*

*Proverbs 11*

**Question**: At some point today give yourself a moment to perform an introspective self-check; are you trustworthy?

Reply/Thoughts:

______________________________________________

______________________________________________

______________________________________________

______________________________________________

______________________________________________

***Author's Notes:***

*In my opinion, I have to say yes. Hopefully, my witnesses would agree.*

***Proverbs 12***

**<u>Question</u>**: How do you interpret the following verse?

9 Better to be an ordinary person with a servant than to be
self-important but have no food.

Reply/Thoughts:

______________________________________________________________

______________________________________________________________

______________________________________________________________

______________________________________________________________

______________________________________________________________

______________________________________________________________

______________________________________________________________

***Author's Notes:***

*Personally, I perceive it to convey; it's better to live humble and willing to teach and guide others than to be merely focused on self and unwilling to lend a helping hand to someone in need. Hear me clearly, my intention was not to re-word this proverb but I did intend to make it personal.*

### *Proverbs 13*

**Question**: An individual with a happy heart is capable of accomplishing many things, but a person with a heavy heart just settles with whatever comes his/her way. Are the dreams of your heart thriving and growing, or are they stagnant?

Reply/Thoughts:

***Author's Notes:***

*Being totally transparent, I can honestly say my dreams are growing and are currently being pursued. I'm faithful that my dreams will one day thrive and accomplish GOD's purpose(s) for my life. Just a quick word to the wise; don't allow anyone, anything, or any situation rob you of your dreams or cause you to live this life heavy-hearted…life is too short! Today, tomorrow, and the years after (GOD willing), breathe breath into your dreams! In my opinion, no two dreams are the same (individually speaking) and I think all dreams have their own unique purpose.*

### *Proverbs 14*

**Question**: Was there a particular verse from today's proverb that caught your attention? If so, which one and why?

Reply/Thoughts:

________________________________________

________________________________________

________________________________________

________________________________________

________________________________________

________________________________________

________________________________________

________________________________________

***Author's Notes:***

*Personally, several verses caught my attention but one in particular caught my eye. "The prudent understand where they are going, but fools deceive themselves."* ***(Proverb 14:8****). Why? Answer: the word "prudent". Allow me to explain by displaying other expressions someone could use in place of the term "prudent"; careful, cautious, sensible, practical, discreet, wise, far-sighted, and having good sense. It has only been through GOD's grace and mercy that He blessed me with a "prudent" spirit. Because for years I deceived myself into believing that I should follow certain paths because I listened to the beliefs of others. That was…until; GOD revealed the path He had always had for me…and I finally listened and decided to obey. Am I perfect? No, but I intend to follow the path laid out for me by the One who is perfect. I thank GOD for a*

*"prudent" spirit!!!*

***Proverbs 15***

**<u>Question</u>**: After reading ***Proverbs 15***, was there a particular verse(s) that really resonated with your spirit/walk at this current time? If so, which one(s) and why?

Reply/Thoughts:

____________________________________________

____________________________________________

____________________________________________

____________________________________________

***Author's Notes:***

*Personally, I would have to say* ***Proverbs 15:14*** *([14] A wise person is hungry for knowledge, while the fool feeds on trash.). Why? Answer: I'm growing more and more cautious of what I choose to consume. I don't know if you've ever heard it before but there's a saying; "You are what you eat" and I don't consider this to be any different. So with that said; if I long for knowledge I should feed myself (mind, body, and soul) with knowledgeable sustenance, rather than with tedious exploits that will only dumb down my awareness of self. I really don't believe there is a need for me to decipher knowledgeable sustenance and tedious exploits, but in case there is; knowledgeable sustenance is something you can use to better yourself and those around you, while tedious exploits are only temporary distractions that may usher in opportunities to spread gossip and leave you feeling malnourished. In essence: the difference between home-cooked meals vs. fast food. Which one is better for you?*

***Proverbs 16***

**<u>Question</u>**: What verse(s) stood out to you in ***Proverbs 16*** and why?

Reply/Thoughts:

***Author's Notes:***

*Personally, two verses stood out to me:*

*"We can make our plans,*
*but the LORD determines our steps."* ***(Proverbs 16:9)***

*"We may throw the dice,*
*but the LORD determines how they fall."* ***(Proverbs 16:33)***

*Why? Answer: Whether we choose to make our own plans or gamble with our lives, in the end…the LORD is in full control. I don't know about you but this gives me great comfort. Regardless of the storm(s) that temporarily drape over my parade or the sunshine that tends to brighten up my day, with the LORD in control blessings can even be found in the midst of rain. If the LORD determines the outcome of my life, may His Will be done and His purpose(s) fulfilled.*

***Proverbs 17***

**<u>Question</u>**: What you think about the highlighted verses?

Reply/Thoughts:

________________________________________________________

***Author's Notes:***

*In my opinion, it shares with me that it is possible for knowledge to exist even in the midst of silence. Personally, I believe it may surprise some people about how much an individual could learn by simply listening rather than talking on some occasions. In addition, I think maintaining an even-temper (transparent moment: this is an area I must work on…specifically, while driving but I'm working on it :-/) will never steer you wrong.*

***Proverbs 18***

**Question**: Have your words been known to be bring life or death (meaning - how do your words impact others)?

Reply/Thoughts:

______________________________________________

***Author's Notes:***

*In my opinion, what you speak…you shall reap and I try to speak life to others even in the most unsuspecting of times. I pray that the LORD will continue to use me as an advocate for His kingdom, because through this particular and personal sacrifice I have found new joy in life. And with this newly found perspective on life, I have discovered the GOD-given inspiration to live life more abundantly. Thank you LORD for your sustaining grace!!!*

***Proverbs 19***

**Question**: What verse in ***Proverbs 19*** grabbed your attention the most?

Reply/Thoughts:

---

***Author's Notes:***

*In my opinion, this proverb didn't hold back any punches at all…nor should it have. There were a number of verses that grabbed my attention, but one in particular grabbed my attention the most: "People ruin their lives by their own foolishness and then are angry at the LORD." (**Proverbs 19:3**). Why? Answer: speaking with complete humility…I used to be guilty of this very thing at times. I would make decisions that I thought were best for me without consulting with the LORD, and then ask Him why things turned out the way they did. I must admit…complete craziness on my part. That's why I'm so thankful today for a greater understanding. GOD saved me; that is overly sufficient enough for me within itself. However, He still continues to provide for His children. As I have grown to realize, in one way or another we will eventually have to make one of two requests; the first one - LORD, direct my steps according to your Will, or the second one - LORD, please help and strengthen me to get back on the right path. From one imperfect person to another, the first request is the much wiser choice. However, if you do find yourself having to make that second request…illustrate your gratefulness by sharing your story with others. Our LORD is truly worthy of praise!!!*

## *Proverbs 20*

There's so much wisdom within ***Proverbs 20*** it's ridiculous (meant in a good way; definitely not bad at all) and I hope you don't read it too lightly. Above, I have highlighted the verses that caught my attention whether it was due to; past experiences, present relevance, or based on the great amount of knowledge that could be found within a particular verse(s). However, I would like to present one in particular for today's study…***Proverbs 20:24***. "The LORD directs our steps, so why try to understand everything along the way?"

**Question**: As believers, if we really allow the LORD to directs our steps…why are we so inquisitive about every minute (*small*) detail?

Reply/Thoughts:

________________________________________________

________________________________________________

________________________________________________

________________________________________________

________________________________________________

________________________________________________

________________________________________________

________________________________________________

________________________________________________

________________________________________________

________________________________________________

________________________________________________

________________________________________________

________________________________________________

________________________________________________

________________________________________________

***Author's Notes:***

*Personally, I believe it all comes back to; how strong our faith is in the LORD. In my opinion, why should we worry about every single pothole along our journey if we have a 24hr roadside assistant who is known to be able to fix any and everything? Trust me; this is speaking to me as well. Thank You LORD for increased knowledge and understanding on a daily basis!!! I give You all the glory!!!*

***Proverbs 21***

Although, there are two particular verses within ***Proverbs 21*** that I could go on and on about…I will refrain, because it's not about me and I aim to live an honorable life. However, there is a verse that I would like to bring to the forefront. "The person who strays from common sense will end up in the company of the dead." (***Proverbs 21:16***).

**Question**: What do you take away from ***Proverbs 21:16***?

Reply/Thoughts:

***Author's Notes:***

*Personally, I took from it that by ignoring the common sense GOD gave us…it could cost us our lives. And not only our physical lives, but our spiritual lives as well. On some occasions, and I've been guilty of this as well, we tend to ignore warning signs and travel down certain paths that could possibly lead to our own destruction. This type of knowledge better helps me understand the importance of good planning, thoughts-before-actions, and preparation explained throughout* ***Proverbs 21****. With that said; I dearly thank the LORD for the common sense He gave me!!!*

***Proverbs 22***

I really believe that we (believers of Christ) are supposed to bring others to Christ and spread the good news (see ***Mark***

***16:15***). By expressing this personal belief, I think the idea of why I chose to highlight ***Proverbs 22:6, 15*** will become more apparent.

**Question**: Is the LORD guiding others through you?

Reply/Thoughts:

***Author's Notes:***

*Personally, I totally agree with the verses highlighted above* ***(Proverbs 22:6, 15)****. Why? Answer: because I've witnessed it myself firsthand and not only have a witnessed it for myself but I have witnessed it in my life as well. Now I'm pretty sure when you read the words "children" and "youngster's" you immediately thought of small kids who are young in age. However, I would like for you to re-evaluate this for a second by reading the following scripture. "Jesus called a little child to him and put the child among them. [3] Then he said, "I tell you the truth, unless you turn from your sins and become like little children, you will never get into the Kingdom of Heaven. [4] So anyone who becomes as humble as this little child is the greatest in the Kingdom of Heaven. [5] "And anyone who welcomes a little child like this on my behalf is welcoming me. [6] But if you cause one of these little ones who trusts in me to fall into sin, it would be better for you to have a large millstone tied around your neck and be drowned in the depths of the sea."* ***(Matthew 18:2-6)****.*

*Regardless of where you are in your personal walk with Christ, we have all been spiritually young and immature at some point…and GOD used someone to teach us the right way (in some cases through the HOLY SPIRIT and not a person). So if the LORD saved you by sending someone, or an advocate* ***(John 14:16-17, 26)****, to physically discipline you (learning how to place spirit above flesh, daily) and what the right path is (following the LORD's direction); why not pass the blessing on to others? If applicable, use this address as a means of motivation. Motivation; to go out and try to reach those who are "spiritually" young (regardless of age) so that when they do mature they won't stray from the right path and they will stay away from foolishness. Thank you LORD for instruction*

*and guidance!!!*

***Proverbs 23***

After reading this proverb all I can say is…wow! I hope everyone reads every verse with an open eye. Especially, ***Proverbs 23:13-14*** (*also look this verse up in other translations as well*); because if parents won't <u>discipline</u> (*not abuse*) their children…the streets, imprisonment, the "system", or the many harsh rigors of life will! Please take note and pass along….

**<u>Question</u>**: Which proverb(s) caught your attention the most?

Reply/Thoughts:

***Author's Notes:***

*Personally, apart from* ***Proverbs 23:13-14, Proverbs 23:4-5*** *what really caught my attention. "Don't wear yourself out trying to get rich. Be wise enough to know when to quit.* [5] *In the blink of an eye wealth disappears, for it will sprout wings and fly away like an eagle." I have discovered through personal experience that wearing yourself out, overtime, I will leave you ineffective…spiritually, mentally, and physically. After many revelations, self-realism, and personal research, I have also discovered; a hard worker is a smart worker…a worker who keeps a "big picture" mentality doesn't become too wrapped in the "here and now". Material things come and go, and most of the time…they leave a lot faster than they come. However, opportunities to help certain individuals come and go and may never come around again. So, make sure you don't tire yourself out too much, because…you never know when the LORD may bring someone your way that needs a little encouragement. Will you have the strength? Today, I can honestly say that I have* ***finally*** *taking heed to these words and it feels good to not be soooo worn out. Thank You GOD for understand and confirmation!!!*

***Proverbs 24***

Although I received my own understanding in regards to the highlighted verses, I don't exactly know who it is for. Take a second and think about your life's current state; do any of them apply? If so, take heed and may GOD bless you through it! If not, perhaps there is someone you may know who can benefit from it, pass it on!

**Question**: What verse(s) resonates with you and why?

Reply/Thoughts:

***Author's Notes:***

*Personally, I would have to say **Proverbs 24: 30-34**. Why? Answer: I have finally recognized that the LORD has a field/ vineyard for me to tend to, and more than ever I must work diligently with a prudent mentality in order to stay away from laziness. **Now** is not a time for me to be caught sleeping; GOD's business is too important and a wonderful harvest waits. For mine enemy comes to steal, kill, and destroy and I must not allow him to catch me sleeping (see **John 10:9-11**).*

***Proverbs 25***

**Question**: Which verse(s) in ***Proverbs 25*** spoke to you today?

Reply/Thoughts:

***Author's Notes:***

*Personally, I would have to say* ***Proverbs 25: 20*** *"Singing cheerful songs to a person with a heavy heart is like taking someone's coat in cold weather or pouring vinegar in a wound" and* ***Proverbs 25:28*** *"A person without self-control is like a city with broken-down walls" spoke to me the most today. I'm reminded to make a conscious effort to understand and respect whatever audience or person that I may cross paths with; so my true intentions aren't seen in the wrong way…helping others and telling them about Christ through personal testimony and faith. In addition, I should never allow myself or someone else to cause me to lose control of myself because if I do…I may become vulnerable to the attacks of the enemy. With these two verses in mind, I pray for discernment. Thank You LORD for revelations!!!*

## *Proverbs 26*

**<u>Question</u>**: What did you take away from ***Proverbs 26***?

Reply/Thoughts:

***Author's Notes:***

*Personally, I took away from it; don't be foolish and don't be lured into it (**v.4-5**), choose to live a life of diligence rather than laziness (**v.13-16**), and don't try to purposely hurt others or initiate chaotic situations (**v.18-19, 24-27**). I believe a lot of trouble and drama can be prevented by just simply stopping to think and choosing to avoid a hasty or haughty tongue. I also think we should make an earnest attempt to keep chaos away from peaceful environments. However, there may come a time when these things can't be avoided…but in the end we can choose how we react. Basically, maintain a life of prudent thought and embrace wisdom. Thank You LORD for clarity!!!*

## *Proverbs 27*

**Question**: Which verse(s) captured your attention?

Reply/Thoughts:

***Author's Notes:***

*The verses highlighted above captured mine. Why? Answer: I'd rather have the sincere thoughts of a "true" friend than the flattering disguised motives of an enemy posing as a real friend. In addition to that; I believe all of this can be discovered by simply finding out what's in a person's heart. But I believe we should kept in mind that just as a person can try to step in a puddle of water and temporarily alter the reflection of an image…the same thing can be applied in the context of* ***Proverbs 27:19****. However, sooner or later the puddle of water will calm and settle then the truth will be clear and certain. I don't who this is for, but I hope it was perceived in the proper context. Don't be so hasty to judge a person or write them off; allow the LORD and time to reveal who that person really is by being level-headed and spiritually calm enough to receive the truth about that person. Thank You LORD for understanding!!*

***Proverbs 28***

**Question**: What verse(s) in ***Proverbs 28*** could you apply to your life and why?

Reply/Thoughts:

***Author's Notes:***

*Personally, I would have to say; "In the end, people appreciate honest criticism far more than flattery."* ***(Proverbs 28:23)****. I'd rather hear an honest truth and become better for it, than to receive an unworthy praise. I give GOD the glory for everything rather than falsely claiming anything for myself. I try to drown my pride in praise daily so that I may grow stronger in my walk. It may sound weird or crazy, but I thank GOD for teaching me humility…because I've learned a lot about myself and others through the process. And for that I'm grateful!*

***Proverbs 29***

**Question**: If you had to choose one verse from ***Proverbs 29*** that affirms your personal testimony…which one would it be?

Reply/Thoughts:

---

***Author's Notes:***

*The verse that affirms my testimony the most is highlighted above;* ***Proverbs 29:6****. I thank GOD for every escape He has given me from sin! Although, I must transparently admit, I didn't always take the chance He gave me to escape. However, I'm grateful for His grace and mercy because He continued to give me a second, a third, and sometimes even a fourth chance to get it right. For this I am truly thankful…thank You LORD!!! And based off of a sermon I received this past Sunday…whatever sin(s) I can't escape from on my own, I ask for the LORD's assistance in removing the sin(s) from my life. Hear me clear when I say, I don't ask for this petition loosely because sometimes transition and progress can hurt. However, I have faith that the end result is truly worth it!! LORD, may Your Will be done!!*

***Proverbs 30***

**Question**: In reference to ***Proverbs 30:29-31***, what do you think prevents "believers" from walking like this for Christ?

Reply/Thoughts:

***Author's Notes:***

*To me, I would have to say it's due to a lack of faith. If a believer has yet to fully grasp or experience* ***Proverbs 30:5*** *firsthand, then I don't believe they will ever be able to walk like that for Christ. In my opinion, a person must be fully persuaded and convinced that the LORD is GOD, before they can walk in full confidence with Him.*

***Proverbs 31***

**Question**: What did ***Proverbs 31*** offer you?

Reply/Thoughts:

______________________________________________

______________________________________________

______________________________________________

***Author's Notes:***

*I don't know about you but this proverb offered me affirmation, conviction, guidance, wisdom, understanding, discipline, and hope. I have a feeling that this proverb will resonate with me well past today, tomorrow, and every day after that LORD willing. I thank GOD for providing clear instruction to a seeking soul! Thank You LORD!!!*

## The Purpose of Proverbs

These are the proverbs of Solomon, David's son, king of Israel.

Their purpose is to teach people wisdom and discipline, to help them understand the insights of the wise.
Their purpose is to teach people to live disciplined and successful lives, to help them do what is right, just, and fair.
These proverbs will give insight to the simple, knowledge and discernment to the young.

Let the wise listen to these proverbs and become even wiser.
Let those with understanding receive guidance by exploring the meaning in these proverbs and parables, the words of the wise and their riddles.

Fear of the Lord is the foundation of true knowledge, but fools despise wisdom and discipline.

***Proverbs 1:1-7***

www.ingramcontent.com/pod-product-compliance
Ingram Content Group UK Ltd.
Pitfield, Milton Keynes, MK11 3LW, UK
UKHW041919190726
13854UKWH00003B/1324

9 781365 569104